Sweet Melon Delights

A Watermelon Jam Cookbook

SWEET MELON DELIGHTS

First edition. February 12, 2024.

ISBN: 979-8224422166

Written by Jose Maria.

Table of Contents

Jose Maria

❖ Introduction to Watermelon Jam

A. History and Significance of Watermelon Jam

Watermelon jam holds a rich history dating back centuries, with its roots tracing back to various cultures across the globe. Historically, watermelon was cultivated in ancient Egypt and was valued not only for its juicy flesh but also for its ability to be preserved as jam. Early recipes for watermelon jam were simple, typically involving sugar and sometimes spices to enhance the flavor.

Throughout history, watermelon jam has been cherished for its ability to capture the essence of summer in a jar. It served as a way to preserve the fruit's freshness long after the harvest season had ended. Watermelon jam also became a staple in many households due to its versatility, used in everything from breakfast spreads to dessert fillings.

In addition to its practical uses, watermelon jam carries cultural significance in various regions. In some countries, it is a symbol of hospitality and is often served to guests as a gesture of welcome and generosity.

B. Health Benefits and Nutritional Value

Watermelon jam not only delights the taste buds but also offers a range of health benefits. Despite its sweet taste, watermelon is low in calories and high in water content, making it a hydrating and refreshing choice. Moreover, it is rich in essential vitamins and minerals, including vitamins A and C, which are important for immune function and skin health.

When watermelon is transformed into jam, it retains many of its nutritional properties, although the sugar content may increase depending on the recipe. However, homemade watermelon jam allows for control over the amount of added sugar, making it a healthier alternative to store-bought jams.

C. Overview of Different Varieties of Watermelon

Watermelon comes in various shapes, sizes, and colors, each with its own unique flavor profile. Some popular varieties of watermelon include:

1. Crimson Sweet: Known for its deep red flesh and high sugar content, the Crimson Sweet watermelon is a favorite for making sweet and flavorful jam.
2. Sugar Baby: This small-sized watermelon is known for its dark green rind and sweet, crisp flesh. It's a popular choice for compact gardens and produces excellent jam.
3. Yellow Doll: With its vibrant yellow flesh and sweet flavor, the Yellow Doll watermelon offers a unique twist on traditional watermelon jam.
4. Moon and Stars: Named for its distinctive yellow spots resembling moons and stars, this heirloom variety boasts a sweet flavor and is ideal for creating visually striking jam.
5. Orangeglo: As the name suggests, the Orangeglo watermelon features bright orange flesh and a sweet, tropical flavor, perfect for adding a burst of color and sweetness to homemade jam.

Each variety brings its own nuances to watermelon jam, allowing for endless possibilities in flavor and texture. Whether you prefer the classic sweetness of Crimson Sweet or the tropical notes of Orangeglo, there's a watermelon variety to suit every palate and culinary creation.

Chapter (1) Getting Started

A. Necessary Equipment and Ingredients

Before diving into the world of watermelon jam-making, it's essential to gather the right tools and ingredients. Here's what you'll need:

Equipment:

1. Large pot or saucepan for cooking the jam
2. Wooden spoon or spatula for stirring
3. Cutting board and knife for preparing the watermelon
4. Blender or food processor (optional, depending on desired consistency)
5. Canning jars and lids for preserving the jam
6. Water bath canner or large pot for processing the jars (if canning)
7. Ladle for filling jars

Ingredients:

1. Fresh, ripe watermelon
2. Granulated sugar or alternative sweetener (such as honey or maple syrup)
3. Lemon juice (for acidity and flavor balance)
4. Pectin (optional, for thickening the jam)
5. Spices or flavorings (optional, depending on the recipe)

B. Tips for Selecting Ripe Watermelons

Choosing the perfect watermelon is crucial for achieving the best flavor and texture in your jam. Here are some tips for selecting ripe watermelons:

1. Look for a Uniform Shape: A ripe watermelon should have a symmetrical shape without any irregularities or dents. Avoid

fruits with bumps or bruises.

2. Check the Field Spot: The field spot is the area where the watermelon rested on the ground while growing. A ripe watermelon will have a creamy yellow or orange field spot, indicating that it's fully matured.

3. Tap for Sound: Give the watermelon a gentle tap with your knuckles. A ripe watermelon will produce a deep, hollow sound. If the sound is dull or flat, the watermelon may be underripe.

4. Inspect the Rind: The rind should be firm and free of soft spots or blemishes. Look for a dull, matte finish rather than a shiny surface, which can indicate an underripe fruit.

5. Consider Weight: A ripe watermelon should feel heavy for its size, indicating that it's full of juice. Lift several watermelons of similar size and choose the heaviest one.

C. Preparing Watermelon for Jam-Making

Once you've selected the perfect watermelon, it's time to prepare it for jam-making. Here's how to get started:

1. Wash the Watermelon: Rinse the watermelon under cool running water to remove any dirt or debris from the surface.

2. Cut and Remove the Rind: Using a sharp knife, carefully cut the watermelon in half. Place each half cut-side down on the cutting board and slice off the rind, working from top to bottom.

3. Remove Seeds (Optional): Depending on your preference, you can either remove the seeds as you cut the watermelon or leave them in for a rustic jam. If desired, use a spoon to scoop out any large seeds.

4. Cube the Flesh: Cut the watermelon flesh into small, uniform cubes. This will help the fruit cook evenly and break down into jam-like consistency.

5. Blend or Mash (Optional): For a smoother jam, transfer the cubed watermelon flesh to a blender or food processor and

pulse until smooth. Alternatively, you can mash the fruit with a potato masher for a chunkier texture.

With your watermelon prepared and ingredients assembled, you're ready to embark on your jam-making adventure!

Chapter (2) Basic Watermelon Jam Recipes

A. Classic Watermelon Jam

Ingredients:

- 6 cups cubed watermelon (about 1 small to medium watermelon)
- 4 cups granulated sugar
- 1/4 cup lemon juice
- 1 tablespoon powdered pectin (optional, for extra thickening)

Instructions:

1. In a large pot, combine the cubed watermelon and sugar. Let the mixture sit for about 1 hour to allow the sugar to draw out the juices from the watermelon.
2. After 1 hour, place the pot over medium heat and add lemon juice. Stir to combine.
3. Bring the mixture to a boil, then reduce the heat to low and let it simmer for 1-1.5 hours, stirring occasionally, until the jam thickens and reaches the desired consistency.
4. If using powdered pectin, dissolve it in a small amount of water and stir it into the jam during the last 5 minutes of cooking.
5. Once the jam has thickened, remove it from the heat and let it cool slightly.
6. Transfer the jam into sterilized jars, leaving about 1/4 inch of headspace. Seal the jars and process them in a water bath canner for 10 minutes (adjust processing time for your altitude if necessary).
7. Allow the jars to cool completely before labeling and storing in a cool, dark place.

B. Watermelon Mint Jam
Ingredients:

- 6 cups cubed watermelon
- 4 cups granulated sugar
- 1/4 cup lemon juice
- 1/4 cup fresh mint leaves, chopped

Instructions:

1. Follow the same instructions as for the Classic Watermelon Jam, combining watermelon, sugar, and lemon juice in a pot and letting it sit for 1 hour.
2. After 1 hour, add the chopped mint leaves to the pot.
3. Proceed with cooking and thickening the jam as directed in the Classic Watermelon Jam recipe.
4. Remove from heat, cool slightly, and transfer to sterilized jars for canning and storage.

C. Watermelon Lemonade Jam
Ingredients:

- 6 cups cubed watermelon
- 4 cups granulated sugar
- 1/2 cup lemon juice
- Zest of 1 lemon

Instructions:

1. Combine watermelon cubes, sugar, lemon juice, and lemon zest in a large pot. Let sit for 1 hour.
2. After 1 hour, bring the mixture to a boil over medium heat, stirring occasionally.

3. Reduce heat and simmer for about 1-1.5 hours, or until the jam thickens to your desired consistency.
4. Remove from heat, cool slightly, and transfer to sterilized jars for canning and storage.

D. Spicy Watermelon Jam
Ingredients:

- 6 cups cubed watermelon
- 4 cups granulated sugar
- 1/4 cup lemon juice
- 1 jalapeño pepper, finely chopped (seeds removed for milder flavor)

Instructions:

1. Combine watermelon cubes, sugar, lemon juice, and chopped jalapeño in a large pot. Let sit for 1 hour.
2. After 1 hour, bring the mixture to a boil over medium heat, stirring occasionally.
3. Reduce heat and simmer for about 1-1.5 hours, or until the jam thickens to your desired consistency.
4. Remove from heat, cool slightly, and transfer to sterilized jars for canning and storage.

Enjoy these delightful variations of watermelon jam on toast, pastries, or as accompaniments to cheese platters and desserts!

Chapter (3) Creative Watermelon Jam Creations

A. Watermelon Jalapeno Jam
Ingredients:

- 6 cups cubed watermelon
- 4 cups granulated sugar
- 1/4 cup lemon juice
- 2 jalapeno peppers, finely chopped (seeds removed for milder flavor)
- 1 teaspoon dried red pepper flakes (optional, for added heat)

Instructions:

1. Combine watermelon cubes, sugar, lemon juice, chopped jalapeno peppers, and red pepper flakes in a large pot. Let sit for 1 hour.
2. After 1 hour, bring the mixture to a boil over medium heat, stirring occasionally.
3. Reduce heat and simmer for about 1-1.5 hours, or until the jam thickens to your desired consistency.
4. Remove from heat, cool slightly, and transfer to sterilized jars for canning and storage.

B. Watermelon Basil Jam
Ingredients:

- 6 cups cubed watermelon
- 4 cups granulated sugar
- 1/4 cup lemon juice
- 1/4 cup fresh basil leaves, chopped

Instructions:

1. Combine watermelon cubes, sugar, lemon juice, and chopped basil leaves in a large pot. Let sit for 1 hour.
2. After 1 hour, bring the mixture to a boil over medium heat, stirring occasionally.
3. Reduce heat and simmer for about 1-1.5 hours, or until the jam thickens to your desired consistency.
4. Remove from heat, cool slightly, and transfer to sterilized jars for canning and storage.

C. Watermelon Berry Fusion Jam

Ingredients:

- 3 cups cubed watermelon
- 2 cups mixed berries (such as strawberries, raspberries, and blackberries)
- 4 cups granulated sugar
- 1/4 cup lemon juice

Instructions:

1. Combine watermelon cubes, mixed berries, sugar, and lemon juice in a large pot. Let sit for 1 hour.
2. After 1 hour, bring the mixture to a boil over medium heat, stirring occasionally.
3. Reduce heat and simmer for about 1-1.5 hours, or until the jam thickens to your desired consistency.
4. Remove from heat, cool slightly, and transfer to sterilized jars for canning and storage.

D. Watermelon Rosemary Jam

Ingredients:

- 6 cups cubed watermelon
- 4 cups granulated sugar
- 1/4 cup lemon juice
- 2 tablespoons fresh rosemary leaves, chopped

Instructions:

1. Combine watermelon cubes, sugar, lemon juice, and chopped rosemary leaves in a large pot. Let sit for 1 hour.
2. After 1 hour, bring the mixture to a boil over medium heat, stirring occasionally.
3. Reduce heat and simmer for about 1-1.5 hours, or until the jam thickens to your desired consistency.
4. Remove from heat, cool slightly, and transfer to sterilized jars for canning and storage.

These creative watermelon jam variations offer unique flavor profiles that are perfect for spreading on toast, pairing with cheese, or using as a glaze for meats and vegetables. Enjoy experimenting with different combinations to find your favorite!

Chapter (4) Using Watermelon Jam in Culinary Applications

A. Breakfast Ideas

Watermelon Jam Pancakes:

- Prepare your favorite pancake batter.
- Heat a skillet over medium heat and lightly grease with butter or oil.
- Pour the pancake batter onto the skillet to form pancakes.
- While the pancakes are cooking, warm the watermelon jam in a small saucepan.
- Once the pancakes are cooked, stack them on a plate and top each pancake with a dollop of watermelon jam.
- Serve hot and enjoy the sweet and fruity twist on traditional pancakes.

Watermelon Jam Yogurt Parfait:

- In a glass or bowl, layer Greek yogurt with spoonfuls of watermelon jam.
- Add granola, nuts, or seeds for crunch.
- Repeat the layers as desired.
- Top with fresh berries or mint leaves for garnish.
- Serve chilled for a refreshing and nutritious breakfast option.

B. Appetizers and Snacks
Watermelon Jam Bruschetta:

- Slice a baguette into rounds and lightly toast them in the oven or on a grill.
- Spread each toast with a generous amount of watermelon jam.
- Top with a slice of fresh mozzarella cheese and a basil leaf.
- Drizzle with balsamic glaze or honey for extra flavor.
- Serve as an elegant appetizer or snack for gatherings.

Watermelon Jam Cheese Board:

- Arrange a selection of your favorite cheeses on a serving board.
- Add small bowls of watermelon jam around the board.
- Include crackers, breadsticks, nuts, and dried fruits for variety.
- Encourage guests to pair the cheeses with the watermelon jam for a sweet and savory combination.

C. Main Course Dishes
Watermelon Glazed Chicken:

- Season chicken breasts or thighs with salt, pepper, and your favorite herbs.
- Grill or pan-sear the chicken until cooked through.
- During the last few minutes of cooking, brush the chicken with warmed watermelon jam to glaze.
- Allow the jam to caramelize slightly on the chicken.
- Serve the watermelon-glazed chicken with a side of salad or roasted vegetables for a summery main course.

Watermelon BBQ Sauce:

- Combine watermelon jam with your favorite barbecue sauce in a saucepan.

- Add a splash of apple cider vinegar and a pinch of chili powder for depth of flavor.
- Simmer the sauce over low heat until heated through and well combined.
- Use the watermelon BBQ sauce to brush onto grilled meats, such as ribs or pork chops, for a sweet and tangy twist on classic barbecue.

D. Desserts

Watermelon Jam Thumbprint Cookies:

- Prepare a basic thumbprint cookie dough.
- Roll the dough into small balls and place them on a baking sheet.
- Use your thumb or the back of a spoon to make an indentation in the center of each cookie.
- Fill each indentation with a small spoonful of watermelon jam.
- Bake according to the cookie recipe instructions until golden brown.
- Allow the cookies to cool before serving.

Watermelon Jam Swirl Ice Cream:

- Soften your favorite vanilla ice cream by letting it sit at room temperature for a few minutes.
- Spoon dollops of watermelon jam onto the softened ice cream.
- Use a knife or spatula to gently swirl the watermelon jam into the ice cream, creating a marbled effect.
- Transfer the ice cream back into the freezer to firm up before serving.
- Scoop into bowls or cones for a refreshing and fruity dessert option.

Chapter (5) Preserving and Storing Watermelon Jam

A. Canning Methods

Canning is a popular method for preserving watermelon jam, allowing it to be stored at room temperature for extended periods. Here's how to can watermelon jam:

1. Prepare the watermelon jam according to your chosen recipe.
2. While the jam is still hot, carefully ladle it into sterilized canning jars, leaving about 1/4 inch of headspace at the top.
3. Wipe the rims of the jars clean with a damp cloth to remove any residue.
4. Place sterilized lids on the jars and screw on the bands until fingertip tight.
5. Process the filled jars in a boiling water bath canner for the recommended time (typically 10 minutes for pint-sized jars, adjust for altitude if necessary).
6. After processing, carefully remove the jars from the canner and place them on a clean towel to cool.
7. Once cooled, check that the lids have sealed properly (the center of the lid should be depressed and not pop up when pressed).
8. Label the sealed jars with the date and store them in a cool, dark place.

B. Freezing Techniques

Freezing is another option for preserving watermelon jam, especially if you prefer not to use canning methods. Follow these steps to freeze watermelon jam:

1. Allow the watermelon jam to cool completely after cooking.

2. Transfer the jam into freezer-safe containers or resealable plastic bags, leaving some space at the top for expansion.
3. Seal the containers or bags tightly to prevent freezer burn.
4. Label the containers with the date and contents.
5. Place the containers in the freezer and store for up to 6-12 months.

When ready to use the frozen watermelon jam, simply thaw it in the refrigerator overnight or at room temperature for a few hours. Once thawed, the jam can be enjoyed as usual.

C. Shelf Life and Storage Tips

Properly preserved watermelon jam can have a shelf life of up to 1 year when stored in a cool, dark place. Here are some additional storage tips:

1. Once opened, store any leftover watermelon jam in the refrigerator. It will keep for several weeks.
2. Always use clean utensils when scooping out jam to prevent contamination.
3. If you notice any signs of spoilage, such as mold growth or off odors, discard the jam immediately.
4. Consider storing smaller jars of watermelon jam for more manageable portions, especially if you don't anticipate using large quantities at once.

By following these preservation and storage methods, you can enjoy the delicious taste of watermelon jam long after the summer season has ended.

Chapter (6) Tips and Troubleshooting

A. Troubleshooting Common Issues

1. Jam not setting: If your watermelon jam doesn't set properly, it may be due to undercooking or not using enough pectin. You can try recooking the jam with additional pectin or lemon juice to help it set.
2. Jam too thick: If your jam turns out thicker than desired, it may have been cooked for too long or too much pectin was added. To fix this, you can stir in a little water or fruit juice to thin it out to your desired consistency.
3. Jam too thin: On the other hand, if your jam is too thin, it may need more cooking time to evaporate excess liquid. You can also add more pectin or simmer the jam at a slightly higher temperature to help it thicken.
4. Sugar crystallization: Sometimes sugar crystals can form in jam, giving it a gritty texture. To prevent this, ensure that the sugar is fully dissolved before bringing the mixture to a boil. You can also add a splash of lemon juice, which helps inhibit crystallization.

B. Tips for Customization and Flavor Variations

1. Experiment with spices: Try adding spices like cinnamon, ginger, or cardamom to your watermelon jam for a warm and aromatic flavor profile.
2. Mix in other fruits: Combine watermelon with other fruits like strawberries, peaches, or pineapple for unique flavor combinations.
3. Add a kick: For a spicy twist, experiment with adding chili peppers, such as jalapenos or habaneros, to your jam.

4. Use different sweeteners: Explore alternatives to granulated sugar, such as honey, maple syrup, or agave nectar, to customize the sweetness of your jam.

C. Creative Serving Suggestions

Charcuterie boards: Serve watermelon jam alongside a selection of cheeses, cured meats, and crackers for a sweet addition to a charcuterie board.

1. Grilled sandwiches: Spread watermelon jam on grilled cheese sandwiches or paninis for a sweet and savory flavor contrast.
2. Salad dressings: Mix watermelon jam with balsamic vinegar and olive oil to create a fruity salad dressing.
3. Cocktail mixer: Use watermelon jam as a cocktail mixer for refreshing summer drinks like margaritas or mojitos.
4. Glazes: Use watermelon jam as a glaze for roasted meats or vegetables, adding a touch of sweetness and flavor to your dishes.

By incorporating these tips and troubleshooting techniques, you can create customized watermelon jam recipes to suit your taste preferences and enjoy them in a variety of creative ways.

Chapter (7) International Watermelon Jam Variations

A. Thai Watermelon Jam with Coconut
Ingredients:

- 6 cups cubed watermelon
- 4 cups granulated sugar
- 1/4 cup lemon juice
- 1 cup shredded coconut (unsweetened)

Instructions:

1. Combine watermelon cubes, sugar, and lemon juice in a large pot. Let sit for 1 hour.
2. After 1 hour, bring the mixture to a boil over medium heat, stirring occasionally.
3. Reduce heat and simmer for about 1-1.5 hours, or until the jam thickens to your desired consistency.
4. Stir in shredded coconut and continue to cook for an additional 5-10 minutes.
5. Remove from heat, cool slightly, and transfer to sterilized jars for canning and storage.

B. Mexican Watermelon Jam with Chili
Ingredients:

- 6 cups cubed watermelon
- 4 cups granulated sugar
- 1/4 cup lime juice
- 2 tablespoons chili powder (adjust to taste)
- 1 teaspoon ground cumin

Instructions:

1. Combine watermelon cubes, sugar, lime juice, chili powder, and ground cumin in a large pot. Let sit for 1 hour.
2. After 1 hour, bring the mixture to a boil over medium heat, stirring occasionally.
3. Reduce heat and simmer for about 1-1.5 hours, or until the jam thickens to your desired consistency.
4. Remove from heat, cool slightly, and transfer to sterilized jars for canning and storage.

C. Greek Watermelon Jam with Ouzo

Ingredients:

- 6 cups cubed watermelon
- 4 cups granulated sugar
- 1/4 cup lemon juice
- 1/4 cup ouzo (Greek anise-flavored liqueur)

Instructions:

1. Combine watermelon cubes, sugar, and lemon juice in a large pot. Let sit for 1 hour.
2. After 1 hour, bring the mixture to a boil over medium heat, stirring occasionally.
3. Reduce heat and simmer for about 1-1.5 hours, or until the jam thickens to your desired consistency.
4. Stir in ouzo and continue to cook for an additional 5-10 minutes.
5. Remove from heat, cool slightly, and transfer to sterilized jars for canning and storage.

These international watermelon jam variations offer unique flavors inspired by different cuisines around the world. Experiment with these recipes to add a global twist to your homemade jam collection.

Chapter (8) Watermelon Jam for Special Diets

A. Vegan Watermelon Jam
  Ingredients:

- 6 cups cubed watermelon
- 1 cup granulated sugar or sweetener of choice (such as maple syrup or agave nectar)
- 1/4 cup lemon juice

Instructions:

1. Combine watermelon cubes and sweetener in a large pot. Let sit for 1 hour.
2. After 1 hour, add lemon juice to the pot.
3. Bring the mixture to a boil over medium heat, stirring occasionally.
4. Reduce heat and simmer for about 1-1.5 hours, or until the jam thickens to your desired consistency.
5. Remove from heat, cool slightly, and transfer to sterilized jars for storage.

B. Gluten-Free Watermelon Jam
Ingredients:

- 6 cups cubed watermelon
- 4 cups granulated sugar
- 1/4 cup lemon juice
- 1 tablespoon powdered pectin (ensure it's gluten-free)

Instructions:

1. Combine watermelon cubes, sugar, and lemon juice in a large pot. Let sit for 1 hour.
2. After 1 hour, add powdered pectin to the pot.
3. Bring the mixture to a boil over medium heat, stirring occasionally.
4. Reduce heat and simmer for about 1-1.5 hours, or until the jam thickens to your desired consistency.
5. Remove from heat, cool slightly, and transfer to sterilized jars for storage.

C. Sugar-Free Watermelon Jam
Ingredients:

- 6 cups cubed watermelon
- 1 cup granulated erythritol or monk fruit sweetener
- 1/4 cup lemon juice
- 1 tablespoon chia seeds (optional, for thickening)

Instructions:

1. Combine watermelon cubes and sweetener in a large pot. Let sit for 1 hour.
2. After 1 hour, add lemon juice and chia seeds to the pot.
3. Bring the mixture to a boil over medium heat, stirring occasionally.
4. Reduce heat and simmer for about 1-1.5 hours, or until the jam thickens to your desired consistency.
5. Remove from heat, cool slightly, and transfer to sterilized jars for storage.

These variations of watermelon jam cater to specific dietary needs, ensuring that everyone can enjoy the delicious taste of homemade jam. Adjust the sweetness and thickness according to your preferences and dietary restrictions.

Chapter (9) Watermelon Jam Cocktails and Beverages

A. Watermelon Jam Mojito
Ingredients:

- 2 tablespoons watermelon jam
- 6-8 fresh mint leaves
- 1/2 lime, cut into wedges
- 2 ounces white rum
- Club soda
- Ice cubes

Instructions:

1. In a cocktail shaker, muddle the watermelon jam, mint leaves, and lime wedges together.
2. Add the white rum and ice cubes to the shaker.
3. Shake well to combine and chill the ingredients.
4. Strain the mixture into a glass filled with ice.
5. Top off with club soda and stir gently.
6. Garnish with a mint sprig and a slice of watermelon, if desired.
7. Serve immediately and enjoy your refreshing Watermelon Jam Mojito!

B. Watermelon Jam Margarita
Ingredients:

- 2 tablespoons watermelon jam
- 1 1/2 ounces tequila
- 1/2 ounce triple sec or orange liqueur
- 1/2 lime, juiced
- Ice cubes

- Salt or sugar (for rimming the glass)
- Lime wedge (for garnish)

Instructions:

1. Rim the edge of a glass with salt or sugar by running a lime wedge around the rim, then dipping it into a shallow dish of salt or sugar.
2. Fill the glass with ice cubes.
3. In a cocktail shaker, combine the watermelon jam, tequila, triple sec, and lime juice.
4. Add ice to the shaker and shake well to combine and chill the ingredients.
5. Strain the mixture into the prepared glass over the ice.
6. Garnish with a lime wedge.
7. Serve immediately and enjoy your Watermelon Jam Margarita!

C. Watermelon Jam Iced Tea
Ingredients:

- 2 tablespoons watermelon jam
- 1 cup brewed black tea, cooled
- 1/2 cup lemonade
- Ice cubes
- Fresh mint leaves (for garnish)
- Watermelon slices (for garnish)

Instructions:

1. In a glass, combine the watermelon jam, brewed black tea, and lemonade.
2. Stir well until the jam is fully dissolved and incorporated into

the liquid.
3.   Fill the glass with ice cubes.
4.   Garnish with fresh mint leaves and watermelon slices.
5.   Stir gently before serving.
6.   Serve chilled and enjoy your refreshing Watermelon Jam Iced Tea!

These delightful watermelon jam cocktails and beverages are perfect for enjoying on a hot summer day or for entertaining guests at your next gathering. Cheers!

Chapter (10) Watermelon Jam Gifts and Packaging Ideas

A. Homemade Jam Jar Labels

1. Personalized Labels: Create custom labels for your watermelon jam jars using printable sticker paper or adhesive labels. Include the name of the jam, ingredients, and a heartfelt message or design.
2. Handwritten Tags: Attach handwritten tags to each jar with twine or ribbon. Write a short message or decorate the tags with doodles or stamps for a rustic touch.
3. Decorative Labels: Use decorative paper or fabric to cover the lids of your jam jars and secure them with a rubber band or ribbon. Add a handwritten label or tag to complete the look.

B. Watermelon Jam Gift Baskets

1. Jam Sampler Basket: Arrange several jars of watermelon jam along with other homemade jams or preserves in a decorative basket. Add crackers, cheese, and a spreader knife for a complete gift.
2. Breakfast Basket: Include a jar of watermelon jam along with pancake mix, maple syrup, and gourmet coffee or tea for a delightful breakfast-themed gift basket.
3. Summer Picnic Basket: Pack a basket with a jar of watermelon jam, artisan bread, cheese, fresh fruit, and a bottle of wine or sparkling water for a perfect picnic outing.

C. Creative Presentation Ideas

1. Mason Jar Decor: Fill mason jars with watermelon jam and tie a fabric square or ribbon around the lid. Add a decorative tag or label for a charming presentation.
2. Mini Jam Bottles: Fill small glass bottles with watermelon jam and seal with a cork or screw cap. Arrange the bottles in a wooden crate or basket for a rustic look.
3. Jar Decorations: Attach decorative charms, beads, or fabric flowers to the lids of your jam jars for a festive touch. Use hot glue or twine to secure the decorations in place.
4. Gift Wrapping: Wrap individual jam jars in colorful tissue paper or cellophane and tie with ribbon or raffia. Add a gift tag or label for a personalized finishing touch.

These creative packaging ideas will elevate your watermelon jam gifts and make them even more special for your friends and loved ones to enjoy.

Chapter (11) Watermelon Jam for Health and Beauty

A. DIY Watermelon Jam Lip Balm
Ingredients:

- 1 tablespoon watermelon jam
- 1 tablespoon coconut oil
- 1 teaspoon beeswax pellets
- 1 teaspoon shea butter
- Optional: a few drops of watermelon seed oil or vitamin E oil for extra nourishment

Instructions:

- In a heat-safe bowl or double boiler, combine the watermelon jam, coconut oil, beeswax pellets, and shea butter.
- Place the bowl over a pot of simmering water or use a double boiler to melt the ingredients together, stirring occasionally until fully melted and combined.
- Once melted, remove from heat and stir in the optional watermelon seed oil or vitamin E oil if desired.
- Pour the mixture into small lip balm containers or empty lip balm tubes.
- Allow the lip balm to cool and solidify at room temperature for a few hours before using.
- Apply the DIY watermelon jam lip balm to your lips whenever needed for soft, hydrated lips with a hint of natural watermelon flavor.

B. Watermelon Jam Face Mask Recipe

Ingredients:

- 2 tablespoons watermelon jam
- 1 tablespoon honey
- 1 tablespoon plain yogurt

Instructions:

1. In a small bowl, combine the watermelon jam, honey, and yogurt.
2. Mix well until all ingredients are thoroughly combined.
3. Cleanse your face and pat dry before applying the face mask.
4. Using clean fingers or a brush, apply an even layer of the watermelon jam face mask to your face, avoiding the eye area.
5. Leave the mask on for 10-15 minutes to allow the ingredients to work their magic.
6. Rinse off the mask with lukewarm water and gently pat your face dry with a soft towel.
7. Follow up with your favorite moisturizer to lock in hydration.
8. Enjoy the refreshed and glowing skin benefits of this nourishing watermelon jam face mask.

C. Benefits of Watermelon Jam for Skin and Hair

1. Hydration: Watermelon jam is rich in water content, making it a hydrating ingredient for both skin and hair. It helps to moisturize dry skin and hydrate parched hair strands.
2. Vitamins and Antioxidants: Watermelon is packed with vitamins A and C, as well as antioxidants, which help to nourish and protect the skin from environmental damage.
3. Exfoliation: The natural enzymes present in watermelon can help to gently exfoliate the skin, promoting a smoother complexion and improving skin texture.
4. Hair Conditioning: When applied to the hair, watermelon jam

can help to condition and soften dry, brittle hair, leaving it more manageable and shiny.

5. Refreshing Properties: The natural fragrance and cooling properties of watermelon make it a refreshing ingredient for skincare products, leaving the skin feeling revitalized and rejuvenated.

Incorporate watermelon jam into your skincare and haircare routine to enjoy its numerous health and beauty benefits, keeping your skin and hair looking and feeling their best.

Chapter (12) Watermelon Jam for Entertaining

A. Hosting a Watermelon Jam Tasting Party

1. Invitations: Send out invitations to your guests inviting them to a watermelon jam tasting party. Include the date, time, location, and any special instructions.
2. Jam Selection: Prepare a variety of watermelon jam flavors for your guests to taste. Offer both traditional and creative variations to appeal to different palates.
3. Tasting Stations: Set up tasting stations with small jars of watermelon jam, along with spoons and crackers for sampling. Label each jam flavor with its name and any relevant information.
4. Accompaniments: Provide a selection of complementary foods to accompany the watermelon jam, such as crackers, bread, cheese, fruit, and charcuterie.
5. Beverages: Offer a variety of beverages to pair with the watermelon jam, including wine, sparkling water, lemonade, and iced tea.
6. Tasting Notes: Encourage guests to take notes on their favorite jam flavors and pairings. Provide pens and notecards or a designated area for recording their thoughts.
7. Entertainment: Enhance the party atmosphere with music, games, or activities related to watermelon or jam-making. Consider hosting a jam-making demonstration or providing DIY jam jar decorating stations.
8. Party Favors: Send guests home with small jars of watermelon jam as party favors, along with recipe cards or tasting notes from the event.

B. Watermelon Jam Pairing Guide with Cheese and Wine

1. Soft Cheeses: Pair watermelon jam with soft cheeses like brie or goat cheese for a creamy and sweet combination.
2. Hard Cheeses: Serve watermelon jam alongside aged cheeses such as cheddar or gouda for a savory and fruity contrast.
3. Wine Pairings: Pair watermelon jam with light-bodied wines such as Riesling or rosé for a refreshing and summery combination. Alternatively, try it with sparkling wine or champagne for a festive twist.
4. Accompaniments: Serve watermelon jam with crackers, bread, or crostini to create delicious bite-sized appetizers. Add nuts, dried fruit, or fresh herbs for additional flavor and texture.

C. Watermelon Jam Party Favors

1. Mini Jam Jars: Fill small jars with watermelon jam and decorate them with ribbon or twine. Attach a personalized tag with a thank-you message for your guests.
2. DIY Jam Kits: Create DIY jam-making kits for your guests to take home. Include a small jar of watermelon jam, a recipe card, and any necessary ingredients or equipment.
3. Jam Jar Decor: Decorate jam jars with colorful fabric or paper and fill them with watermelon jam. Add a handwritten label or tag for a personal touch.
4. Jam-themed Gifts: Pair watermelon jam with other jam-themed gifts such as homemade scones or biscuits, tea towels, or jam spreaders for a thoughtful and practical party favor.

Hosting a watermelon jam tasting party is a fun and memorable way to entertain guests while showcasing the delicious versatility of this summery spread. Whether you're pairing it with cheese and wine or sending guests home with personalized party favors, watermelon jam is sure to delight and impress your guests.

Chapter (13) Farm-to-Table: Growing and Harvesting Watermelons

A. Tips for Growing Watermelons at Home

1. Choose the Right Variety: Select a watermelon variety that is well-suited to your climate and growing conditions. Some popular varieties include Crimson Sweet, Sugar Baby, and Charleston Gray.

2. Provide Plenty of Sunlight: Watermelons thrive in full sunlight, so choose a sunny spot in your garden with at least 6-8 hours of direct sunlight per day.

3. Prepare the Soil: Watermelons prefer well-draining soil with a pH of 6.0-6.8. Amend the soil with compost or well-rotted manure before planting to improve fertility and drainage.

4. Plant at the Right Time: Plant watermelon seeds or transplants outdoors after the last frost date in your area, when soil temperatures have warmed to at least 70°F (21°C). In cooler climates, start seeds indoors several weeks before transplanting outdoors.

5. Provide Adequate Space: Watermelon vines require plenty of space to spread out, so plant them at least 3-4 feet apart in rows or hills. If space is limited, consider growing smaller bush varieties or using trellises to support the vines.

6. Water Regularly: Keep the soil consistently moist but not waterlogged, especially during hot, dry weather. Water deeply at the base of the plants to encourage strong root development.

7. Mulch: Apply a layer of organic mulch, such as straw or shredded leaves, around the base of the plants to help retain moisture, suppress weeds, and regulate soil temperature.

8. Control Weeds and Pests: Keep the garden area free of weeds, which compete with watermelon plants for nutrients and water.

Monitor for common pests such as aphids, cucumber beetles, and squash bugs, and use organic pest control methods as needed.

9. Support Growing Fruit: As watermelon fruits develop, support them with slings made from old pantyhose or fabric strips tied to trellises or stakes. This helps prevent the fruit from touching the ground and reduces the risk of rot.

10. Harvest at the Right Time: Watermelons are ready to harvest when the tendrils near the fruit turn brown, and the underside of the fruit changes from white to yellow. Thump the watermelon—it should sound hollow when ripe.

B. Harvesting and Storing Fresh Watermelons

1. Timing: Watermelons are typically ready for harvest 80-90 days after planting. Harvest in the morning when temperatures are cooler for the best flavor and texture.

2. Cutting: Use a sharp knife or shears to cut the watermelon from the vine, leaving a few inches of stem attached to the fruit.

3. Inspect for Ripeness: Look for signs of ripeness such as a dull, matte appearance on the rind, a yellow or cream-colored spot on the underside, and a hollow sound when thumped.

4. Storing: Store harvested watermelons in a cool, dry place out of direct sunlight. Whole watermelons can be kept at room temperature for up to a week or refrigerated for longer storage. Once cut, wrap leftover watermelon tightly in plastic wrap and refrigerate for 3-4 days.

C. Sustainable Watermelon Farming Practices

1. Crop Rotation: Rotate watermelon crops with other plant families to reduce soil-borne diseases and pests and maintain soil fertility.

2. Cover Cropping: Plant cover crops such as legumes or grasses during the off-season to prevent soil erosion, improve soil structure, and add organic matter.

3. Drip Irrigation: Use drip irrigation systems to deliver water directly to the base of plants, reducing water waste and minimizing weed growth.

4. Integrated Pest Management (IPM): Implement IPM strategies such as crop rotation, beneficial insect habitat enhancement, and the use of organic pesticides as a last resort to manage pests while minimizing environmental impact.

5. Soil Health: Test soil regularly for nutrient levels and pH balance, and amend as needed with organic fertilizers and soil amendments to promote healthy plant growth and fruit development.

6. Pollinator Habitat: Create habitat for pollinators such as bees and butterflies by planting flowering plants around the watermelon field. This encourages natural pollination and supports biodiversity.

By following these tips for growing, harvesting, and storing watermelons at home or on a sustainable farm, you can enjoy delicious, freshly harvested fruit while promoting environmental stewardship and soil health.

Chapter (14) Watermelon Jam in Cultural Traditions

A. Watermelon Jam in Southern Cuisine

Watermelon jam holds a special place in Southern cuisine, where it is cherished for its sweet flavor and versatility. In the Southern United States, watermelon jam is often enjoyed in the following ways:

1. Biscuits and Jam: Watermelon jam is commonly spread on freshly baked biscuits for a delicious breakfast or snack.
2. Pork Glaze: Watermelon jam makes a flavorful glaze for grilled or roasted pork dishes, adding a hint of sweetness and acidity.
3. Accompaniment to Cheese: Serve watermelon jam alongside cheese boards or charcuterie platters for a delightful sweet and savory combination.
4. Dessert Toppings: Use watermelon jam as a topping for ice cream, pound cake, or shortbread cookies for a summery twist on classic desserts.

B. Watermelon Jam in Asian Desserts

In Asian culinary traditions, watermelon jam is used in a variety of sweet treats and desserts, adding a burst of fruity flavor. Some popular uses of watermelon jam in Asian desserts include:

1. Mooncakes: Watermelon jam is sometimes used as a filling for traditional Chinese mooncakes, adding sweetness and moisture to the dense pastry.
2. Taiwanese Shaved Ice: Watermelon jam is drizzled over shaved ice along with condensed milk and fruit toppings for a refreshing and colorful dessert known as "baobing" in Taiwan.
3. Japanese Wagashi: Watermelon jam can be incorporated into Japanese wagashi, or traditional sweets, such as yokan (sweet

bean jelly) or dorayaki (red bean pancakes), for a modern twist on classic recipes.

4. Fruit Sundaes: Layer watermelon jam with other fruits, ice cream, and toppings to create elaborate fruit sundaes popular in many Asian countries.

C. Watermelon Jam in African Culinary Heritage

1. Watermelon jam has also found its way into African culinary heritage, where it is used in both sweet and savory dishes. In African cuisine, watermelon jam is enjoyed in the following ways:

2. Preserves: Watermelon jam is often made as a way to preserve the summer harvest for year-round enjoyment, similar to other fruit preserves used in African cooking.

3. Sauces and Marinades: Watermelon jam can be used as a base for sauces and marinades in African cuisine, adding sweetness and depth of flavor to meat and vegetable dishes.

4. Breads and Pastries: Watermelon jam may be used as a filling for breads, pastries, or turnovers, adding a touch of sweetness to baked goods enjoyed throughout the continent.

5. Condiment for Meats: Watermelon jam can be served alongside grilled or roasted meats, providing a sweet and tangy contrast to savory dishes.

In each of these cultural traditions, watermelon jam adds its own unique flavor and character, showcasing the versatility of this beloved fruit in culinary practices around the world.

Chapter (15) Watermelon Jam in Art and Literature

A. Watermelon Jam in Paintings and Artwork

Watermelon jam, as a symbol of summertime and sweetness, has inspired artists and appeared in various paintings and artworks throughout history. Some examples include:

- Still Life Paintings: Watermelon jam often features in still life paintings depicting tables laden with fruits, desserts, and culinary delights. Artists use vibrant colors and intricate details to capture the lusciousness of the jam and its surrounding elements.
- Genre Paintings: Artists sometimes depict scenes of people enjoying picnics or gatherings where watermelon jam is served alongside other foods. These genre paintings capture moments of leisure and conviviality, with watermelon jam adding a touch of indulgence to the scene.
- Illustrations: Watermelon jam may appear in illustrations for cookbooks, recipe cards, or food advertisements, enticing viewers with its delectable appearance and inviting them to indulge in its sweet flavor.

B. Watermelon Jam in Poetry and Literature

Watermelon jam, with its summery sweetness and nostalgic appeal, has also found its way into poetry and literature, where it serves as a symbol of fond memories, joy, and indulgence. Some examples include:

- Descriptive Poetry: Poets often use vivid imagery and sensory language to evoke the taste, texture, and aroma of watermelon jam. They may describe the sensation of spreading jam on toast or the delight of biting into a freshly baked pastry filled with jam.

- Narrative Prose: Authors sometimes incorporate watermelon jam into their narratives as a recurring motif or symbol. Whether it's a homemade jam shared among friends or a special treat enjoyed on a hot summer day, watermelon jam adds depth and richness to the storytelling.

- Children's Literature: Watermelon jam frequently appears in children's books and stories, where it represents innocence, joy, and the simple pleasures of childhood. Characters may embark on adventures centered around making jam or sharing it with friends and family.

C. Watermelon Jam in Pop Culture References

Watermelon jam has made occasional appearances in pop culture, including film, television, music, and advertisements. Some notable references include:

- Film and Television: Watermelon jam may be mentioned or featured in scenes set during picnics, family gatherings, or holiday celebrations. It adds authenticity to the setting and helps create a sense of nostalgia for viewers.

- Music and Lyrics: Some songwriters incorporate references to watermelon jam in their lyrics, using it as a metaphor for sweetness, love, or indulgence. These references add layers of meaning and emotion to the music, resonating with listeners on a personal level.

- Advertisements: Watermelon jam has been used in advertising campaigns for food products, kitchen appliances, and household goods. Its vibrant color and tempting flavor make it a popular choice for showcasing products in commercials and print ads.

Overall, watermelon jam's presence in art and literature reflects its enduring appeal as a symbol of summer, nostalgia, and the simple pleasures of life. Whether portrayed in paintings, celebrated in poetry, or referenced in pop culture, watermelon jam continues to captivate and inspire audiences around the world.

Chapter (16) Watermelon Jam Preservation Techniques

A. Dehydrating Watermelon for Jam Making

Dehydrating watermelon is a unique preservation technique that concentrates its flavors, making it an excellent base for flavorful watermelon jam. Here's how to dehydrate watermelon for jam making:

1. Prepare the Watermelon: Start by selecting a ripe watermelon and cutting it into small cubes or slices, removing the rind and seeds.

2. Dehydrate the Watermelon: Arrange the watermelon pieces in a single layer on dehydrator trays, leaving space between each piece for air circulation. Set the dehydrator to a low temperature (around 135°F or 57°C) and allow the watermelon to dehydrate for 8-12 hours, or until it is fully dried and leathery in texture.

3. Check for Dryness: Periodically check the watermelon pieces for dryness throughout the dehydration process. They should be firm and dry to the touch with no moisture remaining.

4. Cool and Store: Once fully dehydrated, allow the watermelon pieces to cool completely before transferring them to airtight containers for storage. Store the dehydrated watermelon in a cool, dry place away from direct sunlight.

5. Make Watermelon Jam: To make watermelon jam using dehydrated watermelon, rehydrate the dried fruit by soaking it in water or fruit juice until softened. Then, proceed with your favorite watermelon jam recipe, adjusting the sweetness and flavorings as needed.

B. Fermenting Watermelon for Unique Flavors

Fermenting watermelon is another innovative technique that can yield unique and complex flavors for jam making. Here's how to ferment watermelon for jam:

1. Prepare the Watermelon: Cut a ripe watermelon into small cubes, removing the rind and seeds as needed.
2. Fermentation: Place the watermelon cubes in a clean, sterilized jar or container. Add a starter culture such as whey, yogurt, or a commercial fermentation culture to kickstart the fermentation process. Alternatively, you can rely on the natural yeasts present on the watermelon skin to initiate fermentation.
3. Fermentation Process: Cover the jar with a clean cloth or lid that allows air to circulate while preventing contaminants from entering. Allow the watermelon to ferment at room temperature for 2-3 days, or until it develops a slightly tangy flavor and fizzy texture.
4. Check for Fermentation: Taste the fermented watermelon periodically to monitor the fermentation process. It should develop a pleasant tanginess and effervescence as it ferments.
5. Make Watermelon Jam: Once the watermelon has fermented to your liking, strain off any excess liquid and transfer the fermented fruit to a saucepan. Add sugar and any desired flavorings such as spices or citrus zest, then cook the mixture over low heat until thickened to your desired consistency.

C. Infusing Watermelon Jam with Herbs and Spices

Infusing watermelon jam with herbs and spices is a simple yet effective preservation technique that adds depth and complexity to the flavor profile. Here's how to infuse watermelon jam with herbs and spices:

1. Choose Your Ingredients: Select fresh herbs and spices that

complement the natural sweetness of watermelon, such as mint, basil, ginger, or cinnamon.

2. Prepare the Watermelon: Cut a ripe watermelon into small cubes, removing the rind and seeds as needed.

3. Infusion Process: Place the watermelon cubes in a saucepan and add your chosen herbs and spices. Common combinations include watermelon-mint, watermelon-basil, or watermelon-ginger. Simmer the mixture over low heat, stirring occasionally, to allow the flavors to infuse into the watermelon.

4. Add Sweetener: Once the watermelon has infused with the herbs and spices, add sugar or sweetener of your choice to sweeten the mixture to your liking. Continue to cook the jam over low heat until it reaches your desired consistency, stirring frequently to prevent sticking or burning.

5. Cool and Store: Allow the infused watermelon jam to cool slightly before transferring it to sterilized jars for storage. Seal the jars tightly and store them in the refrigerator for short-term use or process them in a water bath canner for long-term storage.

These preservation techniques offer creative ways to extend the shelf life of watermelon while enhancing its flavor and versatility for jam making. Whether you choose to dehydrate, ferment, or infuse watermelon, you can enjoy delicious homemade jam year-round.

Chapter (17) Watermelon Jam Community and Events

A. Watermelon Jam Festivals Around the World

Watermelon jam festivals are vibrant celebrations of culture, food, and community, showcasing the versatility and deliciousness of this beloved summertime treat. Here are some notable watermelon jam festivals held around the world:

1. Watermelon Festival in Hope, Arkansas, USA: This annual festival celebrates all things watermelon, including watermelon jam competitions, tastings, and demonstrations. Visitors can enjoy live music, arts and crafts vendors, and family-friendly activities.

2. Watermelon Jam Festival in Chinchilla, Queensland, Australia: Held in the "melon capital" of Australia, this festival features watermelon-related competitions, including jam-making contests, as well as live entertainment, carnival rides, and market stalls.

3. Watermelon Festival in Karpuzatan, Turkey: This traditional festival celebrates the watermelon harvest with music, dance, and of course, plenty of watermelon-based dishes and treats, including watermelon jam served with traditional Turkish breads and cheeses.

4. Watermelon Festival in Cordele, Georgia, USA: Known as the "Watermelon Capital of the World," Cordele hosts an annual watermelon festival featuring jam-making demonstrations, seed-spitting contests, and a variety of watermelon-themed activities for all ages.

5. Watermelon Jam Festival in Maule, Chile: This festival celebrates Chilean watermelon production with live music, food stalls, and agricultural displays. Visitors can sample a

variety of watermelon products, including jams, juices, and desserts.

B. Online Watermelon Jam Communities and Forums

In addition to in-person events and festivals, there are also online communities and forums dedicated to watermelon jam enthusiasts. These platforms provide a space for sharing recipes, tips, and inspiration for making and enjoying watermelon jam. Some popular online communities include:

1. Watermelon Jam Facebook Group: This Facebook group brings together watermelon jam lovers from around the world to share recipes, photos, and stories about their jam-making adventures.
2. Watermelon Jam Subreddit: The Watermelon Jam subreddit is a community-driven forum where users can discuss all things related to watermelon jam, including recipes, techniques, and troubleshooting tips.
3. Watermelon Jam Instagram Hashtag: By following the #watermelonjam hashtag on Instagram, users can discover a wealth of photos and posts featuring delicious watermelon jam creations from home cooks and food bloggers alike.
4. Watermelon Jam Pinterest Boards: Pinterest is a treasure trove of watermelon jam recipes and inspiration, with countless boards dedicated to showcasing creative ways to use this summertime favorite in jams, desserts, and more.

C. Hosting Watermelon Jam Making Workshops

Hosting watermelon jam making workshops is a fun and educational way to bring together members of the community to learn new skills and share in the joy of preserving seasonal produce. Here are some tips for hosting a successful workshop:

1. Choose a Venue: Select a venue with ample space for participants to work comfortably, such as a community kitchen, church hall, or outdoor pavilion.

2. Gather Supplies: Stock up on all the necessary ingredients and equipment for making watermelon jam, including fresh watermelon, sugar, jars, lids, and canning tools.

3. Prepare Recipes: Choose a variety of watermelon jam recipes to showcase during the workshop, including classic flavors as well as creative variations with herbs, spices, and other fruits.

4. Demonstrate Techniques: Lead participants through the jam-making process step by step, demonstrating proper techniques for cutting, cooking, and canning watermelon jam.

5. Encourage Participation: Encourage participants to get hands-on experience by inviting them to help with tasks such as chopping fruit, stirring the jam, and filling jars.

6. Share Tips and Tricks: Offer tips and tricks for successful jam making, such as how to test for gel stage, prevent crystallization, and safely process jars for long-term storage.

7. Provide Tasting Samples: Allow participants to sample different varieties of watermelon jam and discuss their flavor profiles and texture.

8. Offer Take-Home Materials: Provide handouts or recipe cards with instructions for making watermelon jam at home, along with resources for further learning and exploration.

By participating in watermelon jam festivals, joining online communities, or attending workshops, individuals can connect with fellow enthusiasts, learn new skills, and celebrate the joy of preserving summer's bounty.

Chapter (18) Watermelon Jam Preservation Techniques

A. Pickling Watermelon Rinds

Pickled watermelon rinds offer a unique and tangy twist on traditional watermelon preservation methods. Here's how to pickle watermelon rinds:

1. Prepare the Rinds: Cut the green outer peel off the watermelon rind, leaving just the white inner portion. Cut the rind into small, uniform pieces, removing any remaining pink flesh.
2. Brine Preparation: In a large pot, combine equal parts water and vinegar (such as white vinegar or apple cider vinegar) along with sugar, salt, and pickling spices (such as mustard seeds, peppercorns, and cloves). Bring the brine to a boil, then reduce the heat and simmer for a few minutes to dissolve the sugar and salt.
3. Pack the Jars: Pack the prepared watermelon rind pieces into sterilized glass jars, leaving a little space at the top. Add any desired flavorings, such as garlic cloves, dill, or chili peppers, to the jars.
4. Pour the Brine: Carefully pour the hot brine over the watermelon rinds in the jars, covering them completely. Use a clean utensil to remove any air bubbles and ensure the rinds are submerged in the brine.

Seal and Store: Seal the jars with sterilized lids and bands, then process them in a water bath canner according to recommended processing times for pickled vegetables. Alternatively, store the pickled watermelon rinds in the refrigerator for short-term use.

Allow to Marinate: Let the pickled watermelon rinds marinate in the brine for at least a week before enjoying. They will develop more flavor and complexity over time.

B. Making Watermelon Jam Syrup

Watermelon jam syrup is a versatile ingredient that can be used in a variety of sweet and savory dishes. Here's how to make watermelon jam syrup:

1. Prepare the Watermelon: Cut a ripe watermelon into small cubes, removing the rind and seeds as needed.

2. Cook the Watermelon: Place the watermelon cubes in a large pot and cook them over medium heat, stirring occasionally, until they break down into a thick, pulpy consistency.

3. Strain the Mixture: Once the watermelon has cooked down, strain the mixture through a fine-mesh sieve or cheesecloth to remove any solids. Press down on the solids to extract as much liquid as possible.

4. Sweeten and Flavor: Return the strained watermelon juice to the pot and add sugar or sweetener of your choice, along with any desired flavorings such as lemon juice, vanilla extract, or fresh herbs.

5. Simmer and Reduce: Bring the mixture to a simmer over medium-low heat, stirring occasionally, and allow it to cook until it thickens into a syrupy consistency. This may take 20-30 minutes or longer, depending on the desired thickness.

6. Cool and Store: Once the watermelon jam syrup has reached the desired consistency, remove it from the heat and allow it to cool completely. Transfer the syrup to sterilized glass bottles or jars for storage. Refrigerate for short-term use or process in a water bath canner for long-term storage.

C. Watermelon Jam Fruit Leather

Watermelon jam fruit leather is a delicious and portable snack that can be made at home with just a few simple ingredients. Here's how to make watermelon jam fruit leather:

1. Prepare the Watermelon: Cut a ripe watermelon into small cubes, removing the rind and seeds as needed.
2. Blend the Watermelon: Place the watermelon cubes in a blender or food processor and blend until smooth. Strain the mixture through a fine-mesh sieve or cheesecloth to remove any seeds or pulp.
3. Sweeten and Flavor: Return the strained watermelon puree to the blender and add sugar or sweetener of your choice, along with any desired flavorings such as lemon juice, lime zest, or mint leaves.
4. Spread the Mixture: Line a baking sheet or dehydrator tray with parchment paper or a silicone baking mat. Pour the watermelon mixture onto the prepared surface and spread it into an even layer, about ¼ inch thick.
5. Dehydrate the Fruit Leather: Place the baking sheet or dehydrator tray in an oven or food dehydrator set to the lowest temperature (around 140°F or 60°C) and allow the watermelon mixture to dehydrate for 6-8 hours, or until it is firm and leathery to the touch.
6. Cut and Roll: Once the watermelon jam fruit leather is fully dehydrated, use a sharp knife to cut it into strips or shapes. Roll up the fruit leather strips and store them in an airtight container at room temperature for up to several weeks.

These preservation techniques offer creative ways to extend the shelf life of watermelon while enjoying its delicious flavor in new and exciting ways. Whether you're pickling watermelon rinds, making watermelon jam syrup, or crafting watermelon jam fruit leather, you're sure to delight in the results.

Chapter (19) Watermelon Jam for Breakfast

A. Watermelon Jam Stuffed French Toast
Ingredients:

- Thick slices of bread
- Watermelon jam
- Eggs
- Milk
- Cinnamon
- Vanilla extract
- Butter or cooking oil

Instructions:

1. Spread watermelon jam generously between two slices of bread to make sandwiches.
2. In a shallow dish, whisk together eggs, milk, cinnamon, and vanilla extract to make the French toast batter.
3. Dip each watermelon jam sandwich into the egg mixture, coating both sides evenly.
4. Heat butter or oil in a skillet over medium heat. Cook the stuffed French toast until golden brown on both sides.
5. Serve hot, optionally topped with powdered sugar, fresh fruit, or maple syrup.

B. Watermelon Jam Breakfast Muffins

Ingredients:

- All-purpose flour
- Baking powder
- Salt
- Sugar
- Eggs
- Milk
- Vegetable oil
- Watermelon jam

Instructions:

1. Preheat the oven to 375°F (190°C) and line a muffin tin with paper liners.
2. In a large bowl, whisk together flour, baking powder, salt, and sugar.
3. In another bowl, beat together eggs, milk, and vegetable oil until well combined.
4. Gradually add the wet ingredients to the dry ingredients, stirring until just combined. Be careful not to overmix.
5. Fill each muffin cup halfway with batter, then add a spoonful of watermelon jam to the center of each.
6. Top with more batter until the muffin cups are about three-quarters full.
7. Bake for 18-20 minutes or until a toothpick inserted into the center comes out clean.
8. Allow the muffins to cool slightly before serving.

C. Watermelon Jam Granola Bars

Ingredients:

- Rolled oats
- Almonds, chopped
- Sunflower seeds
- Coconut flakes
- Honey or maple syrup
- Watermelon jam
- Coconut oil
- Salt

Instructions:

1. Preheat the oven to 350°F (175°C) and line a baking pan with parchment paper.
2. In a large bowl, combine rolled oats, chopped almonds, sunflower seeds, coconut flakes, and a pinch of salt.
3. In a saucepan, heat honey or maple syrup, watermelon jam, and coconut oil until melted and well combined.
4. Pour the wet mixture over the dry ingredients and stir until everything is evenly coated.
5. Press the mixture firmly into the prepared baking pan, using the back of a spatula or your hands to compact it.
6. Bake for 20-25 minutes or until golden brown and set.
7. Allow the granola bars to cool completely before cutting into bars or squares.

These breakfast recipes offer delicious ways to incorporate watermelon jam into your morning routine, whether you prefer sweet stuffed French toast, wholesome muffins, or satisfying granola bars.

Chapter (20) Watermelon Jam Around the World

A. Watermelon Jam in Mediterranean Cuisine:

Watermelon jam is cherished in Mediterranean cuisine for its refreshing sweetness and versatility. In this region, watermelon jam is often enjoyed in the following ways:

1. Traditional Breakfast Spreads: Watermelon jam is commonly spread on toast, croissants, or biscuits for a sweet and indulgent breakfast treat.
2. Accompaniment to Cheese: Watermelon jam pairs beautifully with a variety of cheeses, such as feta or goat cheese, creating a delightful sweet-savory contrast on cheese boards or appetizer platters.
3. Dessert Enhancer: Watermelon jam is used as a filling for pastries, cakes, and desserts, adding moisture, flavor, and vibrant color to baked goods.
4. Condiment for Savory Dishes: Watermelon jam can also be used as a glaze or sauce for grilled meats, roasted vegetables, or savory tarts, lending a touch of sweetness and acidity to savory dishes.

B. Watermelon Jam in Caribbean Delicacies:

In Caribbean cuisine, watermelon jam adds a tropical flair to a variety of dishes and beverages. Here's how it's enjoyed:

1. Tropical Cocktails: Watermelon jam is often used as a key ingredient in refreshing cocktails and mocktails, such as rum punches, daiquiris, and fruit spritzers, providing a burst of sweet watermelon flavor.
2. Condiment for Jerk Chicken: Watermelon jam makes a

delicious accompaniment to spicy jerk chicken, offering a cooling contrast to the heat of the dish and enhancing its tropical flavors.

3. Dessert Toppings: Watermelon jam can be drizzled over desserts like ice cream, sorbet, or coconut rice pudding for a sweet and fruity finish.

4. Fusion Cuisine: Watermelon jam is sometimes incorporated into fusion dishes that blend Caribbean and international flavors, such as watermelon-glazed ribs or watermelon salsa served with seafood.

C. Watermelon Jam in Pacific Islander Dishes:

In Pacific Islander cuisine, watermelon jam is appreciated for its natural sweetness and ability to complement traditional flavors. Here are some ways it's used:

1. Island Breakfast Spreads: Watermelon jam is commonly spread on toast, pancakes, or breakfast pastries as a sweet and flavorful topping to start the day.

2. Accompaniment to Tropical Fruits: Watermelon jam pairs well with a variety of tropical fruits, such as pineapple, mango, and papaya, in fruit salads, smoothie bowls, or fruit tarts.

3. Traditional Treats: Watermelon jam may be used as a filling for traditional Pacific Islander desserts, such as coconut turnovers, breadfruit pies, or taro puddings, adding sweetness and moisture to these delicacies.

4. Refreshing Beverages: Watermelon jam can be dissolved in water or coconut water to make refreshing drinks, or mixed with lime juice and mint for a tropical agua fresca.

In each of these culinary traditions, watermelon jam contributes its unique flavor and versatility, enhancing a wide range of dishes and beverages enjoyed throughout the Mediterranean, Caribbean, and Pacific Island regions.

Chapter (21) Watermelon Jam Crafts and DIY Projects

A. Watermelon Jam Scented Candles:

Watermelon jam scented candles offer a delightful way to bring the sweet aroma of summer into your home. Here's how you can make them:

Ingredients and Supplies:

- Soy wax flakes or beeswax pellets
- Candle wicks
- Candle dye or crayons (red and green)
- Watermelon fragrance oil or essential oil
- Heat-resistant jars or containers
- Double boiler or microwave-safe bowl
- Stirring utensil
- Thermometer

Instructions:

1. Begin by melting the soy wax flakes or beeswax pellets in a double boiler or microwave-safe bowl according to the package instructions.
2. Once the wax is fully melted, add a few drops of red candle dye or grated red crayon to achieve a watermelon pink color. Stir well to distribute the color evenly.
3. Add a few drops of watermelon fragrance oil or essential oil to the melted wax and stir to incorporate the scent.
4. Secure the candle wicks to the bottom of your jars or containers using a dab of melted wax.
5. Carefully pour the scented wax into the jars, leaving some space at the top.
6. Allow the candles to cool and harden completely before

trimming the wicks to the desired length.

7. Optionally, you can create a green wax layer on top to mimic the rind of a watermelon. Melt green candle dye or crayon and pour a thin layer over the pink wax once it has cooled and solidified.

8. Once the candles have fully set, they are ready to be enjoyed. Light them up and let the sweet scent of watermelon fill the air!

B. Watermelon Jam Handmade Soap:

Watermelon jam handmade soap not only cleanses but also leaves your skin smelling fresh and fruity. Here's how to make it:

Ingredients and Supplies:

- Clear glycerin soap base
- Watermelon fragrance oil or essential oil
- Red and green soap dye
- Soap molds
- Microwave-safe bowl
- Stirring utensil
- Spray bottle filled with rubbing alcohol (optional)

Instructions:

1. Cut the clear glycerin soap base into small cubes and place them in a microwave-safe bowl.

2. Melt the soap base in the microwave in short bursts, stirring frequently to ensure even melting.

3. Once the soap base is fully melted, add a few drops of watermelon fragrance oil or essential oil and stir well to combine.

4. Divide the melted soap base into two portions. Add red soap dye to one portion and green soap dye to the other, mixing until you achieve the desired watermelon colors.

5. Pour the green soap mixture into the soap molds, filling them

about halfway. Allow this layer to cool and harden slightly.

6. Once the green layer has set, pour the red soap mixture on top to create the watermelon "flesh." Leave some space at the top for the green "rind."

7. Allow the soap to fully harden and cool in the molds. You can speed up this process by placing the molds in the refrigerator for about 30 minutes.

8. Once the soap is completely set, carefully remove it from the molds. If desired, lightly spritz the soap with rubbing alcohol to remove any air bubbles and give it a smooth finish.

9. Your watermelon jam handmade soap is now ready to use or gift to friends and family who will love its sweet scent and nourishing properties!

C. Watermelon Jam Fabric Dye Techniques:

Using watermelon jam as a natural fabric dye can create beautiful, soft shades of pink and red. Here's how to dye fabric with watermelon jam:

Ingredients and Supplies:

- White or light-colored fabric (such as cotton or linen)
- Watermelon jam
- Large pot or saucepan
- Water
- White vinegar
- Rubber gloves
- Stirring utensil

Instructions:

1. Begin by prewashing the fabric to remove any dirt, chemicals, or finishes that may interfere with the dyeing process.

2. In a large pot or saucepan, combine watermelon jam with water

in a ratio of about 1 part jam to 4 parts water. Add a splash of white vinegar to help set the dye.

3. Place the pot on the stove and heat the mixture until it reaches a simmer. Stir occasionally to dissolve the jam and distribute the color evenly.

4. Once the dye bath is simmering, add the prewashed fabric to the pot, ensuring that it is fully submerged. Use tongs or a stirring utensil to agitate the fabric and promote even dye absorption.

5. Allow the fabric to simmer in the dye bath for at least 1-2 hours, stirring occasionally to ensure consistent coloration.

6. After the desired dyeing time has elapsed, carefully remove the fabric from the dye bath and rinse it thoroughly under cold water until the water runs clear.

7. Hang the dyed fabric to dry in a well-ventilated area away from direct sunlight. Once dry, the fabric can be laundered as usual to remove any excess dye residue.

8. Your watermelon jam dyed fabric is now ready to be used in sewing projects, quilting, or crafting, adding a unique touch of color and character to your creations.

These watermelon jam-inspired crafts and DIY projects offer creative ways to incorporate the sweet and vibrant essence of watermelon into your home decor, personal care routine, and creative endeavors. Enjoy the process and the sweet results!

Chapter (22) Watermelon Jam for Pets

Watermelon jam can be a delightful and nutritious treat for pets when used appropriately. Here are some ways to incorporate watermelon jam into your furry friends' lives:

A. Homemade Watermelon Jam Dog Treats:
Ingredients:

- 2 cups diced seedless watermelon
- 1 tablespoon honey (optional)
- 1/4 cup plain yogurt (optional)

Instructions:

1. Place the diced watermelon in a blender or food processor and blend until smooth.
2. If desired, add honey for sweetness and yogurt for creaminess, then blend again until well combined.
3. Pour the mixture into ice cube trays or silicone molds.
4. Freeze the treats for a few hours until firm.
5. Once frozen, pop the treats out of the molds and store them in an airtight container in the freezer.
6. Give your dog one of these refreshing treats on a hot day as a cool and hydrating snack.

B. Watermelon Jam Catnip Infused Toys:
Ingredients and Supplies:

- Catnip
- Fabric scraps or old socks
- Sewing kit or fabric glue
- Watermelon jam (for scent)

Instructions:

1. Sprinkle dried catnip onto a small piece of fabric or into an old sock.
2. Add a small amount of watermelon jam to the fabric or sock to entice your cat with the scent.
3. Fold the fabric or sock and secure it with a few stitches or fabric glue to create a toy.
4. Present the catnip-infused toy to your cat for hours of playful enjoyment.

C. Watermelon Jam for Small Animals:

For small animals such as rabbits, guinea pigs, or hamsters, watermelon jam can be offered in small amounts as an occasional treat. Ensure that the watermelon jam does not contain any added sugars, artificial sweeteners, or preservatives, as these can be harmful to small animals. Additionally, always introduce new foods slowly and monitor your pet for any adverse reactions.

When feeding watermelon jam to pets, moderation is key. While watermelon is safe for most pets in small quantities, too much can cause digestive upset or diarrhea. Always consult with your veterinarian before introducing new treats or foods into your pet's diet, especially if your pet has any underlying health conditions or dietary restrictions.

With these homemade treats and toys, you can incorporate the delicious flavor of watermelon jam into your pets' lives in a safe and enjoyable way. Just remember to monitor your pets while they enjoy these treats and adjust the recipes as needed to suit their preferences and dietary needs.

❖ Conclusion

A. Final thoughts on watermelon jam:

Watermelon jam is a versatile and delicious treat that captures the essence of summer in a jar. With its vibrant color, sweet flavor, and refreshing taste, watermelon jam adds a burst of sunshine to any meal or snack. Whether enjoyed on toast for breakfast, paired with cheese for a savory appetizer, or incorporated into desserts and beverages, watermelon jam is sure to delight the taste buds and brighten the day. Plus, its natural sweetness makes it a healthier alternative to store-bought jams and spreads, providing a guilt-free indulgence for those with a sweet tooth.

B. Encouragement for further experimentation:

As you continue your culinary journey with watermelon jam, don't be afraid to get creative and experiment with new flavors, ingredients, and techniques. Try adding herbs like mint or basil for a refreshing twist, or spices like ginger or cinnamon for a warming kick. Mix watermelon jam into salad dressings, marinades, or cocktails for a unique flavor boost, or use it as a topping for grilled meats or roasted vegetables. The possibilities are endless, so let your imagination run wild and see where it takes you!

C. Resources for additional recipes and inspiration:

For more watermelon jam recipes and inspiration, consider exploring the following resources:

1. Online recipe websites and food blogs: Websites like Allrecipes, Food Network, and Bon Appétit often feature a wide variety of watermelon jam recipes, along with user reviews and ratings to guide your culinary adventures.
2. Cookbook collections: Check out your local library or bookstore for cookbooks dedicated to preserving and canning, as well as those focusing on fruit-based recipes. You may find

some hidden gems waiting to be discovered!

3. Social media and online communities: Join online groups or forums dedicated to home cooking, canning, and preserving. Platforms like Reddit, Facebook, and Pinterest are great places to connect with fellow food enthusiasts, share recipes, and exchange tips and tricks.

4. Farmers' markets and local produce stands: Visit your local farmers' market or farm stand during watermelon season to find fresh, ripe watermelons perfect for making homemade jam. Chat with the vendors for insider tips on selecting the best fruit and get inspired by the seasonal bounty.

Remember, the joy of cooking lies not only in the end result but also in the process of discovery and experimentation. So have fun, embrace your inner chef, and savor every delicious moment with watermelon jam!